Avelino Marcos Guarienti

Credit cooperatives and socio-economic development

Avelino Marcos Guarienti

Credit cooperatives and socio-economic development

Credit as a means of promoting the growth and development of the medical profession

ScienciaScripts

Imprint
Any brand names and product names mentioned in this book are subject to trademark, brand or patent protection and are trademarks or registered trademarks of their respective holders. The use of brand names, product names, common names, trade names, product descriptions etc. even without a particular marking in this work is in no way to be construed to mean that such names may be regarded as unrestricted in respect of trademark and brand protection legislation and could thus be used by anyone.

Cover image: www.ingimage.com

This book is a translation from the original published under ISBN 978-3-330-77046-1.

Publisher:
Sciencia Scripts
is a trademark of
Dodo Books Indian Ocean Ltd. and OmniScriptum S.R.L publishing group

120 High Road, East Finchley, London, N2 9ED, United Kingdom
Str. Armeneasca 28/1, office 1, Chisinau MD-2012, Republic of Moldova, Europe
Managing Directors: Ieva Konstantinova, Victoria Ursu
info@omniscriptum.com

Printed at: see last page
ISBN: 978-620-8-63109-3

SUMMARY

DEDICATORY

To my family, for the attention given to me, for the affection I received at times when I needed to continue with my studies, for their understanding and words of comfort when I couldn't hide my worries and difficulties. Thank you very much.

To my fellow students, for your friendship, companionship and, above all, for the good times we had together, because without that, everything would have been more difficult. Thank you for being together.

To my colleagues at Unicred Planalto Médio, for understanding how important it was for me to complete this course and for their help on the days and times when I needed to be away.

To the management of Unicred Planalto Médio, for the support, encouragement and words of encouragement I received. You were very important in making this course a reality. Thank you.

To the professors at Unisinos, for the valuable knowledge they imparted.

SUMMARY

The aim of this work is to systematically show society in general the importance of Credit Cooperatives, providing information on how they operate, detailing their main activities and specificities, their benefits and advantages compared to the traditional financial system. To this end, quantitative data from the Unicred System in Brazil is presented, which shows that, in addition to the growth of this important segment of credit, initially aimed at medical activity and, more precisely, at health professionals today, it carries out its main activity, financial intermediation, raising and lending funds among its cooperative members and carrying out its most important function, which is to foster their activity and, consequently, bring about the social and economic development of the class. To reinforce the contextualization of the work, a survey was carried out among the members of the Cooperativa de Crédito dos Médicos do Planalto Médio do RS - Unicred Planalto Médio RS, located in the city of Passo Fundo - RS, with the aim of diagnosing their level of participation and satisfaction with the services provided by the cooperative. The results showed that, on average, 96.14% of members are satisfied with the way the cooperative operates and the activities it carries out.

INTRODUCTION

Consistent with its origins, cooperatives have shown over time that no force can be ignored. For this reason, and in this regard, what must be considered is that no person who is willing to work and add their skills to the development of activities allied to working in a cooperative can be left out. Therefore, everyone has the right to participate, align themselves with the doctrine and enjoy its benefits.

Cooperativism is effective when it is well managed, in whatever field of activity it operates. For this reason, and as society's knowledge of the cooperative movement grows, its growth is inevitable, with new fronts for action in the market, increasing the number of members and consolidating the principles of mutual aid.

Thus, the doctrine is being confirmed day after day, creating work alternatives for millions of people around the world, because cooperatives have such a positive impact on society that we clearly believe that it is the state that needs the cooperative, and not the other way around, because it creates alternatives for social inclusion.

The existence, on the part of bodies linked to cooperatives, such as OCB, OCE's and SESCOOP, of programs that bring knowledge about the cooperative movement to communities, especially young people, cooperative members, employees and administrators, means that the movement is growing significantly every day.

This work presents, in detail, the branch of Credit Cooperativism, an activity that is going through a moment of affirmation and consolidation, since, as we intend to show, it is a model that fits in all areas and serves to tackle the country's socio-economic problems.

In recent years, credit unions have seen significant growth, mainly due to the current government's response to long-standing demands, which have encouraged the sector, such as the Central Bank of Brazil's publication of new regulations, which will be discussed in the course of this article, and which have led to this increase.

In addition, its main activity, the promotion of credit, is available to its members, increasing the general development of society, either by raising and applying funds, or, above all, by guiding its members towards a change in the paradigm of pure competition, towards a fairer and more solidary form of economy, seeking to achieve economic development, not just capitalist, but socially-oriented, because with credit available to members and at a lower cost than that practiced by the market, it suggests possibilities for new investments.

It is well known that, although in Brazil the dissemination of the values of this new way of uniting society in pursuit of a common goal reaches only a part of the population, and is still a subject of wide discussion among peoples, it has been fundamental in promoting development and integration, especially in emerging countries. Brazil itself, which for many years benefited and still benefits from international cooperation, has been developing cooperation programs with developing countries for over 20 years.

For your information, in Brazil, when it comes to credit unions, there have been movements of growth and shrinkage over time. Decades ago, in a phase of growth, the so-called *Luzzatti* cooperatives were created, which were free to join and which, over time, went through a process of shrinkage, due to the lack of preparation of the administrators for the proper conduct of the business, since they served different social classes and policies aimed at greater control of their activities. Article 3, sole paragraph, of Resolution 1.914 of 11/03/1992 disallowed the creation of new *Luzzatti-type* cooperatives, which still operate today, but in very small numbers.

We are currently experiencing a new phase of expansion. With the issuance of CMN Resolution No.° 3.321[1] of September 30, 2005, which reintroduced the admissibility of free cooperatives, but with a series of conditions, such as: the necessary affiliation to a central cooperative; the creation of additional control mechanisms and; the accountability of their managers, the government is trying to avoid the mistakes of the past.

With the introduction of this measure, the government has signaled that cooperatives could be an important part of the social context, given the possibility of democratizing credit in the country. If this happens, the main beneficiaries will be ordinary citizens, who will be able to invest their resources and take out loans, whether for rural or urban enterprises. And all this for their own benefit and that of the community, because the cooperative is their own business.

In the development of this work, we will try to show, specifically, the current model of credit cooperativism and, more precisely, the way in which the Unicred Planalto Médio - RS Credit Cooperative operates, how it is inserted into society and its benefits for its members.

It is in this context that we will try to analyze and identify the activities carried out by this cooperative segment, because, in addition to being a subject of extreme importance today, it will also be of great value to the reader who is interested in getting to know it.

1 Provides for the incorporation, authorization to operate, operation, amendments to the bylaws and cancellation of authorization of Credit Cooperatives and for external audits of single credit cooperatives.

1 DELIMITATION OF THE PROBLEM AND ITS JUSTIFICATION

One of the major concerns of the Credit Cooperative System is the search for member loyalty. In this context, what happens is that, despite the advantages offered by Credit Unions, a significant portion of the members, according to surveys and information from the leaders of these institutions, do not operate, or do not move all of their financial resources with the institution.

If Credit Unions, due to the way they operate, have different characteristics from other financial institutions, especially when it comes to financial intermediation (raising and investing funds), offering comparative advantages to their members, there is an internal market to be conquered.

Brazilian credit cooperatives are undoubtedly growing. And this can be clearly seen, not only in the numbers, which are significant, but also in the concept of cooperative members and society as a whole, which is becoming more interested than ever in getting to know it.

By gaining a significant foothold in Brazil's financial system, credit unions are increasingly seeking to provide their members with comparative advantages over traditional banks, either by raising funds or by investing those funds through loans and financing at lower interest rates, thereby boosting their members' activities and increasing their income.

Nowadays, if the vast majority of the Brazilian population is still unfamiliar with a Credit Union and its specificities, at least at some point they have heard of it or obtained some service from it.

For your information, at Unicred Planalto Médio, the administration (board members and management) is not professionalized, dedicates only part of its time to running the administration and, as determined by the bylaws, does not receive any fees. In this respect, emphasis is placed on the fact that the entire membership, over time, makes its contribution to the cooperative and, through this activity, can not only gain technical knowledge about the overall functioning of the financial system, its laws, functions and activities, but also seek information about conducting business.

The aim of this work is to systematically provide the members of the cooperative being researched, the Unicred conglomerate and other sectors of society with information on how a credit union operates, its peculiarities, its benefits, its functions and its advantages and disadvantages compared to the traditional financial system.

In addition, to diagnose the following with members, through research and quantitative data:

- Are the objectives for which the Credit Cooperative - Unicred Planalto Mèdio RS was created and which are described in Article 2 of its Bylaws, which aim to provide financial advantages in relation to the local financial system, being achieved?

- through financial intermediation, more precisely through the promotion of credit, with attractive interest rates and greater ease in contracting, has there been growth, and at what level, of the medical profession covered by the cooperative?

- what is the level of participation and satisfaction of the members in relation to the management and activities carried out by the cooperative?

This is what is presented, and what we intend to answer during the course of this work, because it is necessary to have an urgent and broad understanding of the subject and so that the reader, despite other interpretations, knows that the creation of a Credit Union is, without a doubt, one of the best ways of promoting the economic and social development of a community.

1.1 General Objective

To analyze the current state of Brazilian credit cooperatives, detailing their segments, their activities, current legislation, their benefits to cooperative members, in order to be able to verify, together with this, through a survey of cooperative members, their level of participation and satisfaction, as well as the real advantages provided by the cooperative and the level of action of cooperative members, in terms of the movement of their resources in the cooperative, both in financial investments and in taking out credit.

1.2 Specific Objective

1) Diagnose, together with the members, the level of competitiveness and the cooperative's capacity to leverage and develop medical activities, both physically and legally;

2) Create a theoretical framework on the activities of a Credit Union and its actions;

3) To assess the interest of members in moving and investing their funds in the cooperative, as well as to find out the percentage of the volume of funds invested by them;

4) To see how interested members are in participating in the management of the cooperative at some point.

2 HISTORICAL CONTEXT OF COOPERATIVISM IN BRAZIL

In order to be able to carry out a more in-depth study on the subject of this work, it is first necessary to know part of the history of Brazilian cooperativism.

It can be seen that between 1830 and 1879 there was a period of experimentation with pre-cooperatives, where various cooperative movements came close to the principles developed by the first cooperative in 1844, in the town of Rochdale, England.

According to studies, the first forms of pre-cooperative organization in Brazil include the "Republic of Palmares", which was formed by slaves and later attracted other ethnic groups. Another form of cooperation, which began in 1610, is linked to the founding of the first Jesuit reductions. Known as the Republic of the Guarani, located in South America, its members established tea, tobacco, honey and corn as their main currency, goods that were traded as if they were money, with their value expressed, fictitiously, in "peso".

Oriented in this way, all production was geared towards satisfying the needs of its members. And in this organizational context, commercial and financial profit, which nowadays burdens the economy in all parts of the world, was excluded, so that the regulatory engine of the market was not established by profit and competition, but by the good of the solidarity community and its property.

Finally, the Guarani Republic, as a form of work and trade organization, existed from 1610 to 1763 and was, as history shows, the first to really practice and carry out cooperative work.

We can also see that the doctrinal principles of cooperativism, implemented in 1844 when the first cooperative was founded by the 28 weavers of Rochdale, England, who were suffering from low wages and poor living conditions, were based on the same guidelines adopted by the Guarani.

According to the literature, cooperatives began in Brazil in 1847, with the founding of the Tereza Cristina colony in the backlands of Paranà. Although it was not a cooperative organization as such, it had a very similar form of community and associative action. Other experiences emerged at the same time, in the neighbouring state of Santa Catarina, inspired by the "falanstério" model, an organization of small communities, made up of no more than 10 families, where all the produce was marketed and the income was shared equally, to everyone's benefit.

From then on, with the cooperative movement growing all over the world as a form of organization capable of reducing the problems between capital and labour, the first legally constituted cooperatives appeared in Brazil in 1891:

- 1891, in Limeira SP, the Cooperative of Telephone Company Employees;
- 1892, in Alfredo Chaves and Antônio Prado RS, the Società Cooperativa delle Convenzioni

Agricoli Industriali. The country's first rural producers' cooperative;

- 1894, in Rio de Janeiro DF, the Military Consumer Cooperative;

- 1895, in Camaragibe PE, another Consumer Cooperative;

- 1897, in Campinas SP, the Consumption Cooperative of the Employees of the Companhia Paulista de Estradas de Ferro;

- 1898, in Ouro Preto, Minas Gerais, the Public Employees' Consumption Cooperative;

Special mention should be made of the founding of the first Rural Credit Cooperative in Brazil and Latin America, inspired by the Raiffeisen model, after several meetings between what we might say were the tireless leaders of the time.

Led by Father Theodoro Amstadt, and attended by 19 members, on December 28, 1902, in the ballroom of Mr. Nicolau Kehl, in Linha Imperial, about 8 km from the headquarters of the district of Nova Petrópolis, in Rio Grande do Sul, the statutes of the cooperative were discussed and approved. The cooperative was called Caixa Rural Cooperativa, later changed to Cooperativa de Crédito Rural de Nova Petrópolis - COOPERURAL.

From then on, several other Rural Credit Cooperatives were founded in Brazil, as well as those for other activities, such as the first Agricultural Cooperatives in the state of Minas Gerais (1907), the Agricultural Cooperative with Credit Section, founded in 1911 in Vila Nova RS, near Porto Alegre, and the Cooperative of Employees of the Viaçao Férrea do RS, founded in 1917.

In addition, there is news of the creation of several cooperatives in the south of Brazil after the crisis of 1929, motivated by the crash of the New York Stock Exchange, which were created with the aim of overcoming the economic problems faced at that time.

In 1932, the first fundamental law on cooperatives was passed with the approval, on December 19 of that year, of Decree No. 22,239, which enshrined the Rochdalian doctrinal basis and guaranteed cooperatives a reasonable margin of freedom to form and operate.

After the introduction of this law, until 1964, the cooperative movement experienced a period of great activity, with the founding of various cooperatives in different segments, such as: agricultural cooperatives , rural electrification, rural credit, consumer credit, urban credit, housing, work and health.

However, between 1964 and 1970, due to changes in legislation and internal disputes, cooperatives experienced a period of crisis, with the consumer and credit cooperatives almost completely disappearing.

After several years of discussion, motivated precisely by the lack of legislation that would, at the time, cover all the wishes of cooperative societies, Law No. 5.764 was enacted on December 16, 1971, which is still in force today and which regulates cooperative societies in Brazil. This law certainly consolidated cooperativism as a movement of great economic and social expression.

Since then, other decrees have been introduced into the cooperative system as a whole, but only to regulate certain relationships between labor and taxation, with a greater emphasis on the introduction of regulatory standards for the credit cooperative system, which will be seen in the course of the work.

3 LITERATURE REVIEW

The main purpose for setting up a Credit Union is the need to provide financial intermediation services to its members, carrying out activities with them and only with them that aim to carry out business that provides a greater return on resources, in addition to ensuring that these activities fall within those determined by its articles of association, i.e. that they are in line with its core activities.

However, if these objectives are to be achieved and Credit Unions are to be able to face up to the changes brought about by the global world, they must not lose sight of the well-established values of cooperativism, such as mutual aid, responsibility, honesty, democracy, education and constant concern for the members. Any change in these values disfigures cooperativism and takes away its credibility.

According to Cattani:

> Cooperatives are autonomous associations of people who come together voluntarily and form a jointly owned company to satisfy economic, social and cultural aspirations. They are based on the values of mutual aid, solidarity, democracy, participation and autonomy. (2003, p.63)

In order to better define the current moment in which cooperativism is living, Carrion and Vizentini say: "The world economy is going through a moment of intensified intercapitalist rivalry (which does not exclude agreements and coalitions, but supposes them) and, in this climate, no protagonist is capable of guaranteeing the position they have won." (1997, p.59)

In this respect, what we can see in our country, despite the existing concerns, is that Credit Cooperatives, especially with the introduction of new policies, developed especially by the monetary authorities (Central Bank of Brazil), have been playing an important role in the country's economic and social development, even establishing their position.

The issuance of CMN Resolution No. 3,106[2] of June 25, 2003, by the Central Bank of Brazil, brought a new and promising stage to Brazilian Credit Cooperativism, which began to be written, pointing the way to socio-economic development, as it authorized the formation of free association Credit Cooperatives in the community. This Resolution was revoked by CMN Resolution No. 3,321/05, also issued by the Central Bank of Brazil, which maintained this authorization and included other instructions, among which were to adapt and maintain more effective control of their activities, especially with regard to the responsibility of their managers in conducting the business.

This resolution has facilitated the process of people joining a cooperative, but not necessarily belonging to homogeneous groups. However, it should be pointed out that this may have the

2 Resolution 3.106 defined the requirements and procedures for the incorporation, authorization to operate and amendments to the bylaws, as well as for the cancellation of authorization to operate of credit cooperatives.

consequence, although not proven, of a possible deterioration in the "spirit" and principles of cooperatives, due to the lack of identity among its members.

However, without a doubt, the possibility of free association has been a significant factor in the evolutionary process of credit cooperatives in Brazil, which, with this measure, is moving towards what is happening today in countries where cooperatives have existed for longer and are more evolved, and are definitely capable of competing with the unbridled competition of capitalism.

After all, according to Cattani, the results of more than two hundred years of dominance by the capitalist mode of production point to the need to build another economy to meet the demands of a more demanding, technically and intellectually qualified society. The need for justice, human respect and better achievements is felt all over the world. Instead of fractious competition, the feelings that emerge strongly in some groups are those of cooperation and solidarity; instead of the devastation of nature, a respectful relationship with multiple forms of life; instead of the process of accumulation and irrational concentration of wealth, the generosity of sharing and giving. (2003, p. 10)

On the other hand, it can be seen that legislation, although it has taken on many positive aspects in recent years, is still one of the factors that has prevented Brazilian credit cooperatives from playing a more prominent role in the economy, capable of sustainably promoting the growth and socio-economic development of the country, its companies and its people.

Credit Unions, like any other, are institutions managed and administered by their members, and it is through self-management, with reduced costs when compared to traditional financial institutions, presenting a lack of bureaucracy in their activities, motivated by the proximity and knowledge of their members and their financial capacity, that they are able to operate short and long-term loans and financing at lower interest rates, allowing investments to be made that can leverage business and increase the income of their members.

In this sense, the search for efficiency and the fight to beat the competition are no longer the sole preserve of commercial companies. Cooperatives of all kinds, especially credit unions, are also engaged in this battle.

In this respect, what we see, according to Cattani, is that: "the financial results as well as the debts are the members' responsibilities and are divided according to the members' turnover." (2003, p. 18)

After all, we mustn't forget that, according to Carrion and Vizentini:

> the international economy lives in a somewhat disordered environment, with little regulatory capacity to resist the growing challenges of the product, financial, exchange and capital markets. Fluctuations in international exchange and interest rates reflect the growing instability of economies and the risks arising from low medium and long-term productive investment. (1997, p.65)

So, what you need to know is that credit unions are the answer to these macroeconomic issues that exist in our country's financial system, which does not fully meet the demands of society because, contrary to what it should be, they are the economic counterpart to the concentration of income itself. Thus, they now play a new and important role, which is to help and defend not only the members who participate in it, but also, indirectly, the entire community.

The Brazilian economy, because of the way it has been run by the government, has developed in a disorganized way, favoring the wealthiest classes, to the detriment of a development model that could bring greater benefits to society.

In this sense, even though the government aims to do the opposite, according to Brum, "The current Brazilian economic development model can be characterized as peripheral, associated, dependent, exporting, concentrating and excluding capitalist." (p.98, 2000)

Despite this interpretation, cooperativism is absolutely part of this activity, because generating jobs and distributing income in a fair and equal way, according to the intellectual and production capacity of each individual, as well as winning markets through competitiveness and competence, is absolutely part of this activity.

If we look for historical information, we'll see that cooperatives, as a form of organization, emerged in 1844, in the midst of the industrial revolution during a crisis in the employment of labor, spreading around the world and becoming one of the most solid bases for socio-economic organization of various social groups. For this reason, the growth of cooperatives in various sectors around the world is the most concrete form of this manifestation.

In Brazil, it resurfaced in the 1990s, also motivated by unemployment. Official figures show that the increase in the formation of new cooperatives between 1990 and 1998, a period of social crisis, is directly related to the rise in unemployment. It can also be seen that this increase in the number of cooperatives, of all kinds, is the result of a social response to the problem of poor income distribution and social injustice, making cooperatives a way of meeting not only the needs of the demand for labor, but also some of the shortcomings of the state's actions, which do not adequately fulfill their functions (allocative, distributive and stabilizing).

For this reason, according to Cattani, "cooperation means taking part in a collective enterprise whose results depend on the action of each of the participants." (2003, p.49)

After all, according to Cattani, "The cooperative establishes relationships with its members that are different from those that capital companies maintain with their suppliers or purchasing clients." (2003, p.68)

So, what we can see is that, more than an alternative, cooperatives, especially credit cooperatives, with their ability to promote activities of interest to their members, which facilitate investments to increase production, can be seen as an excellent solution to the serious problem of unemployment that afflicts the entire planet. Furthermore, there is no economic activity that cannot be organized through the principles of cooperativism.

Also, with regard to the development of our country, according to Brum:

> The development model in force in the country is exclusionary because, by orienting and stimulating the economy primarily to meet the demands of the upper class and for exports, and by creating and activating mechanisms of repression, it excludes millions of Brazilians from the national historical process, who continue to be in a situation of absolute or relative economic, social, political, cultural and educational marginality. (p.125, 2000)

According to Brum: "The realization of development implies the existence of a project for life and a project for society. A people only assumes its destiny to the extent that it manages to define its own national project." (p.125, 1982)

In the words of Lesbaupin, when referring to Brazil: "The concentration of income is probably the most determining factor in the high level of poverty, since the country has the eighth highest income in the world, a rich endowment of factors and an average level of per capita income." (1999, p.51-52)

It remains to be seen that association, in the form of cooperation, is undoubtedly the most appropriate way to find solutions to combat unemployment and the high concentration of income and, in this context, credit unions have sought to play a fundamental role in the search for a fairer and more equal society.

After all, as seen above, cooperatives are associations of people and according to Cattani, associationism is nothing more than "the process by which one or more people and/or group(s) decide to come together on a regular basis, but not necessarily continuously, to meet common demands." (2003, p.15)

In the same vein, in the words of Cattani:

> The association or partnership of two or more people goes beyond the conclusion of a mutual contract that establishes obligations aimed at common objectives. The essence of this civil society is based on the sharing of profits, the union of efforts and the establishment of another type of collective action, which has qualified cooperation as the implementation of another type of social action. (2003 p.15)

3.1 Identifying principles of cooperativism

In order to carry out a study on any topic that has the cooperative system as its object, be it of any activity, it is necessary to verify the cooperative principles, since it is through them that we can identify which directions the organization should take during its future business trajectory.

In this sense, and in order to be able to verify more clearly the content dealt with in this work, it is necessary to carry out research on the aforementioned principles, so that we can, in addition to drawing some conclusions on the subject, identify whether the cooperative researched is properly framed in the cooperative doctrine.

Therefore, we describe below the seven current cooperative principles adopted at the Congress of Manchester, England, held in September 1995 by the International Cooperative Alliance - ICA, the most representative cooperative organization in the world, which encompasses 705 million cooperative members, which we will now analyze.

3.1.1 Free and voluntary membership

In studying this principle, we see that it contains the old "open door" principle, encompassing the rule of voluntariness, mentioned by the post-Rochdalian doctrine, as described by Cattani:

> Cooperatives are voluntary organizations open to all people able to use their services and willing to accept their responsibilities as members, without gender, social, racial, political or religious discrimination. (2003, p.63)

This principle can be seen in two ways, the positive and the negative. The positive preaches that membership is free, i.e. it should be open to all, provided they make use of its services and accept the responsibilities related to their membership, and voluntary, as it depends exclusively on the will of the cooperative member. The negative aspect refers, more precisely, to the denial of the existence of artificial restrictions on the entry of new members, accepting restrictive circumstances.

However, it is a mistake to interpret the principle of free membership to mean that all cooperatives are obliged to accept all membership applications. Cooperatives have no legal duty to accept them. It is therefore the cooperative's right to restrict the free entry of new members.

On this principle, it can be seen from the Credit Union's side that the current legislation, Resolution 3.321/05, in its article 9, I and II, makes it clear that only people who comply with the bylaws and practice the same related, complementary or correlated activities can be admitted to the cooperative's membership.

3.1.2 Democratic control by shareholders

At the Manchester Congress, the following was noted in relation to this cooperative principle:

> Cooperatives are democratic organizations, controlled by their members, who actively participate in establishing their policies and making decisions. Men and women, elected as representatives, are responsible to the members. (CATTANI. 2003, p. 63)

This principle establishes the democratic method for choosing directors, who assume responsibility towards those who chose them. Democratic management presupposes not only a single vote, but also the participation of cooperative members in all the activities of the cooperative, on an equal footing with other members. It also establishes that, in singular cooperatives, members have equal conditions for choosing their managers and for making decisions on the items on the agenda of general meetings, i.e. one member, one vote.

3.1.3 Economic participation of the partner

This principle expresses one of the pillars of cooperatives, the Share Capital, because unlike traditional companies, in addition to being democratically controlled by the members, it can receive, according to the decision of the Ordinary General Meeting, compensation from the previous year's surpluses, which, although limited to the subscribed capital, increases it, increasing business conditions and, consequently, enabling the institution to develop further.

For a better understanding, Cattani states that:

> The members allocate the profits for the following purposes: development of the cooperative, making it possible to establish reserves, part of which may be indivisible; returns to the members in proportion to their transactions with the cooperatives; and support for other activities approved by the members. (2003, p.64)

In this respect, it can be seen that Brazilian legislation deals with the issue clearly, when it specifies the mandatory allocation of part of the net surpluses, to the constitution of Reserve Funds, which is intended to repair losses and meet the development of the cooperative's activities, FATES - Technical, Educational and Social Assistance Fund, intended to provide assistance to members, their families and, when provided for in the articles of association, to the cooperative's employees, consisting of a minimum of 5% and a maximum of 10% of the profits. The remainder may be allocated to other funds of a specific nature, or to distribution to cooperative members, in proportion to their operations with the company.

In addition, it should be noted that the surpluses or leftovers produced by the operations of a cooperative, if any, belong to the members and should be distributed in such a way as to avoid them obtaining differentiated gains.

The legislation also stipulates that the distribution of losses at the end of the financial year must be made proportionally to the members, in accordance with the same rules for using the cooperative's services.

3.1.4 Autonomy and independence

Cooperatives, by their nature and purpose, in addition to being institutions of mutual aid, are autonomous, since the members have the right to determine their actions, their destiny, their organization and the way they act in the market, but always in accordance with the cooperative law in force, with a view to their development.

In this respect, according to Schneider, apud, Münkner, H.H., autonomy means:

> a) the autonomy of the members to determine the objectives of their common actions, without any imposition or external interference; b) the autonomy of the members to draft and modify the statutes, in accordance with what the law allows;

c) the autonomy to choose the representatives who will be the administrators, to whom the members will delegate the powers necessary for democratic administration and control; d) the autonomy of the Executive Board to implement the cooperative's policy and to run the business, in accordance with the statutes and the criteria of an agile, flexible and efficient administration; e) the autonomy of the individual cooperatives vis-à-vis the integrated structures, since these structures in cooperatives are formed organically from the grassroots towards the top and not vice versa; therefore, objectives, guidelines, etc. cannot be imposed "from above". cannot be imposed "from the top down", but must be the result of free discussion and decision making on the part of the first-level cooperatives in relation to their integrated structures (federations, centrals, confederations, state, national and international cooperative organizations). (2003, p.202)

Thus, in a simple analysis, this principle is not only of fundamental importance, it is also part of the essence of cooperation and an indispensable element of cooperative societies.

3.1.5 Education, training and information

According to the ICA, the development of education is no longer an accessory or optional principle for cooperatives, which are obliged to promote the education of their members, employees and managers, with a view to better integrating them so that the objectives can be achieved.

As can be seen from the study carried out, with regard to the existing concerns on the subject, more precisely, the need for internal training, regardless of its staff, be they members, directors, advisors or employees, and with regard to the external plan, with a view to reaching the public in general. Education must cover technical aspects, but it must also take into account various other factors, such as the doctrine and the associative and business aspects of cooperative life.

Education can be considered a "fuel" that feeds cooperativism, and contributes significantly to the success of the other principles.

In Schneider's words: "cooperative education is an ongoing process that transcends the limits of formal, institutionalized education that takes place through schools and universities." (2003, p.134)

In Brazil, education is currently fostered institutionally by the legal obligation laid down in Law 5.764/71, which established the obligation to withhold 5% (five percent) of the cooperative's profits to set up FATES - the Technical, Educational and Social Assistance Fund.

3.1.6 Cooperation between cooperatives

This principle is basically linked to the legal permission given to cooperatives so that, if they are interested, they can associate with other cooperatives at the same level in order to expand their business and achieve their social objectives, always with the aim of better serving their members.

In this sense, the ICA's approach to the subject is as follows: "Cooperatives, in order to better serve the interests of their members and their communities, should collaborate by all means with other cooperatives at the local, national and international levels." (NAMORADO, apud ACI, 1966).

The study found that there are two types of cooperative inter-cooperation: informal and federative dynamics.

The first, according to Namorado, "translates into a web of contractual ties that reflect economic or other types of collaboration, more or less regularly, and which do not imply the loss of the individuality of each cooperative". (1995, p.95).

In other words, cooperatives practice mutual aid without having to compete with each other.

In the case of dynamic federative inter-cooperation, according to Namorado, "it leads to the grouping of cooperatives into higher-level structures, whatever their nature and whatever their name". (1995, p. 95).

Thus, first-level cooperatives (singular) must be associated with second-level cooperatives (centrals) and these, in turn, with third-level cooperatives (federations and confederations), since there is a need, in view of the services they provide, for administrative, accounting and legal advice.

In addition to the above principles, the International Cooperative Alliance (ICA) introduced a seventh principle at the Maschester Congress in 1995, which refers to "Concern for the Community". The international cooperative system now has seven principles. For a better understanding, let's take a look at the new principle.

3.1.7 Community Concern

This principle has been given great importance, which is necessary for cooperative societies to be able to develop actions aimed at the growth and development of the communities where they operate, through measures aimed at expanding their activities, obviously always taking into account their social objectives.

It was with this concern in mind that, according to Becho, the ICA drafted the concept of this principle as follows: "Cooperatives work for the sustainable development of their communities through policies approved by their members" (1999, 2nd ed. p.121)

There is not much to add as to what the introduction of this principle might mean for the cooperative system, except for what has already been described above, that is, the expansion of the activities of existing cooperative societies vis-à-vis their communities, although the real context introduced by the ICA is obvious, since the people who set up a cooperative do so in the interest of meeting a need in the region where they operate, there are other fields of activity in which cooperatives should participate.

Therefore, according to Cattani: "Cooperatives work for the sustainable development of their communities through policies approved by their members". (2003, p. 64)

In this sense, the decision to introduce this principle is perhaps best suited to drawing the attention of the authorities to allowing the cooperative system as a whole to have greater power to act, enabling them to compete with greater bargaining power in the market in general and, in this way, to be able to work towards the sustainable development of the communities in which they operate.

3.2 Legislation

In Brazil, the first legislation dealing with cooperatives was Legislative Decree No. 979 of January 6, 1903, which allowed unions, among other authorizations, to organize rural agricultural credit banks, as well as production or consumer cooperatives, without detailing the matter.

Since then, a number of other decrees and laws have been issued to keep up with developments in the sector. Currently, the law that governs cooperatives as a whole in Brazil is Law 5.764, of December 16, 1971, which, when it was issued, revoked Decree-Law 59, of November 21, 1966, as well as Decree 60.597, of April 19, 1967.

The scope of Law 5.764/71, although it deals with a wide range of issues relating to cooperatives, is currently quite out of date in relation to the sector's current needs.

There are several aspects of the law that need to be better assessed and revised. For this reason, the latest version of the bill, after several revisions, is currently before Congress for approval, where it is hoped that it will meet the sector's wishes.

In addition, we have Law 10.406 of January 10, 2002, which establishes the new Civil Code. This law, which is much more recent than 5.764/71, deals with cooperative societies in Chapter XII. Although the chapter is quite short, containing only four articles, it deals with the characteristics of cooperatives and the responsibilities of their directors:

Art. 1.093: Cooperative societies shall be governed by the provisions of this Chapter, with the exception of special legislation.

Art. 1.096: Where the law is silent, the provisions relating to simple companies shall apply, subject to the characteristics set out in Art. 1.094.

The chapter added little to Cooperativism, as it brought little or nothing new, however the legislator did not forget the sector and this, in itself, is extremely important.

On the other hand, in relation to Credit Unions, the main subject of this paper, several Resolutions have been issued by the National Monetary Council.

Among the most important, and why not say extremely important, is Resolution 1,914 of March 11, 1992, which was issued, revoking Resolutions 11, 27 and 99. This resolution, in addition to containing the rules for the establishment and operation of Credit Cooperatives, giving new impetus and impetus to the sector, brought in its article 3, sole paragraph, the prohibition of the establishment of Credit Cooperatives of the "luzzatti" type, thus understood as those without restriction of members, and establishing as basic types for granting authorization for operation the mutual savings and credit cooperatives and the rural credit cooperatives.

After the issuance of other resolutions aimed at meeting the demands of credit cooperatives, including Resolutions 2.771/00 and 3.058/02, Resolution 3. 106 of 06/25/2003 was issued.106 of 25/06/2003, which had as its major evolution in relation to the previous ones, the authorization for the creation of free admission cooperatives, returning the permission that had been revoked by Resolution 1.914/92 that prevented the creation of "luzzatti" type Credit Cooperatives.

Currently we have Resolution 3.321 of September 30, 2005, which revoked Resolution 3.106/03, consolidating the rules issued by that resolution and bringing other important changes, specifically in relation to the obligation for singular cooperatives to be affiliated to a central cooperative, as well as the creation of additional control mechanisms and the accountability of their managers, with a view to properly conducting business and following other rules, including the Resolutions:

a) 2.025/93, which amends and consolidates the rules on opening, maintaining and operating deposit accounts;

b) 2.099/93, which approves the regulations that provide for the conditions regarding access to the National Financial System, the installation of branches and the obligation to maintain minimum values relative to Adjusted Net Worth, in an amount commensurate with the degree of risk of the active operations of financial institutions and other institutions authorized to operate by the Central Bank of Brazil;

c) 2.554/98, which provides for the implantation and implementation of an internal control system;

d) 2.682/99, which deals specifically with the criteria for classifying credit operations and the rules for setting up provisions for doubtful debts;

e) 2.804/00, which deals with risk and liquidity control systems;

f) 2.837/01, which defines the Reference Equity of financial institutions and other institutions authorized to operate by the Central Bank of Brazil;

g) 2.878/01, which provides for procedures to be observed by financial institutions and other institutions authorized to operate by the Central Bank of Brazil when contracting operations and providing services to clients and the public in general;

h) 3.041/02, which establishes conditions for holding office in statutory bodies of financial institutions authorized to operate by the Central Bank of Brazil;

i) 3.198/04, which amends and consolidates the regulations on the provision of independent auditing services for financial institutions, other institutions authorized to operate by the Central Bank of Brazil and for clearing houses and providers of clearing and settlement services.

In addition, one cannot fail to mention the rules applied by the Federal Revenue Office, which relate more specifically to the tax treatment of credit cooperatives.

Thus, on June 23, 2003, Normative Instruction No. 333 was issued, which provides for income tax levied at source on income earned by Credit Cooperatives and paid or credited to their members.

This Instruction consists of just four articles:

Art. 1 Financial investments made by Credit Unions in other non-cooperative financial institutions are not characterized as cooperative acts, and income tax is levied on the result obtained by the cooperative in these investments;

Art. 2 - Withholding income tax is waived on the income referred to in the previous article;

Art. 3 - Income from fixed-income and variable-income financial investments, subject to this condition, paid or credited by Credit Unions to their members, as a result of investments they make in the latter, is subject to withholding tax;

Art. 4 This Normative Instruction comes into force on the date of its publication.

In this way, what we see is that, in relation to taxation, the Federal Revenue Office has also established its rules to govern the financial movement of Credit Unions' idle resources, raised from their members.

4 COOPERATIVES AS A TOOL FOR SOCIAL DEVELOPMENT

In recent years, cooperative societies have played an important role in the economic and social development of the classes and communities in which they operate.

This role is clearly evident when we see, above all, the introduction of the doctrine into the educational system and, more precisely, even with the creation of educational cooperatives, showing that, with this tool, we believe in the development of children and young people with a cooperative vision, who can carry out, in the future, work aimed at economic growth and development, not only capitalist, but also, and above all, socially-oriented.

The 1988 Constitution ended the phase of state intervention and gave Brazilian cooperatives a glimpse of a new horizon, with better conditions for self-management. With the beginning of this new cycle, Brazilian cooperatives were forced to adapt to the new times and had to urgently seek to professionalize their management in order to serve their members and the market more efficiently.

In our country, the development and growth of cooperatives has been constant in recent years and, more precisely, at the present time, due to the great social exclusion of individuals from the means of production, a fact that can be seen in the accelerated growth of cooperatives in various branches.

However, although cooperatives have been occupying a prominent place in the market in all the segments in which they operate, the current legislation is deficient, which is one of the factors that has prevented the sector from playing a more prominent role in the economy, promoting growth and the socio-economic development of the country and its people.

After all, cooperatives are, as we have seen in the historical context, considered an alternative for combating economic and social inequality and, more precisely, by going against the capitalist logic and becoming an important form of organization for needy social segments, especially in periods of unemployment and economic recession.

In this respect, it can be seen that, due to the inefficient actions of the state and economic agents, due to a lack of interest or capacity to make investments, especially in the social area, cooperatives have been growing and expanding in various areas, albeit in a disorganized way, due to the lack of strategic knowledge on the part of the people who manage them, in order to meet the demand for social services required by a significant portion of the underprivileged population.

In addition, today, in the new globalized market economy, there is also a new world conflict, where countries are not using weapons, missiles or nuclear artifacts, but rather instruments that promote a war of markets, without borders or countries, and the protagonists of all this are us, who participate in it.

The unbridled quest for efficiency and the struggle to overcome imperfect competition are no longer the privilege of commercial companies alone. Cooperatives of all kinds are also engaged in this battle.

Cooperatives generate employment, especially in the labor cooperative sector, and are the economic counterpart to income concentration. They are therefore playing a new and important role in Brazil's economic development.

After all, generating jobs and distributing income fairly and equally, according to the intellectual and production capacity of each individual, as well as winning markets through competitiveness and competence, is part of cooperative activity.

Thus, cooperativism, if well structured, is undoubtedly one of the most important forms of social economy, as it is known as the solidarity economy. If we study this concept in more depth, we'll see that in Europe, for example, social economy is the same as cooperativism.

Therefore, more than an alternative, cooperativism is presented as the solution to the serious problem of unemployment that afflicts the entire planet, especially in our country. Moreover, what we have seen so far is that there is no economic activity that cannot be organized through the principles of cooperativism.

And it is in order to provide better living conditions for individuals in society, both in social and economic terms, that various social movements have sought a form of organization based on cooperation.

A clear example of this reality is the rural settlements, where the cooperative doctrine, if used well, is seen as essential for the viability of individuals' socio-economic lives. The way in which these people act, as they seek a better position in society, both personally and for their families, must be based on the principles of cooperatives, because only in this way will they be able to make the production system viable, making solidarity prevail, with the participation of all the cooperative members in an organized way.

In this context, we can also see the growth of work cooperatives, which are seen by an increasing number of people, generally without professional qualifications, as an alternative for obtaining employment and income. In recent years, work cooperatives have been one of the fastest-growing segments of Brazilian cooperativism and in the most diverse sectors of the economy, such as: transport, construction, public entities, etc...

This growth is undoubtedly part of the major restructuring that has been taking place in the national and international economy, motivated by the excessive concentration of income. We know that the introduction of new technologies, which require new working methods, specific knowledge and organization of production, is one of the factors that causes the most unemployment. In this way, the well-known labor market, based on subordinate employment and, more precisely, on salaried work, is being disrupted.

In the face of this competitive environment and increasing demands for quality, the companies that control the markets in ever smaller numbers have reduced their workforce and will continue to do so.

Another important detail, which has stimulated and is still a reason for the creation of new work cooperatives, is the lower tax burden levied on this type of association, which is seen as a strong instrument of flexibility between capital and labor.

Thus, associationism, in the form of cooperation, is undoubtedly the most appropriate way to find solutions to combat unemployment and the high concentration of income, improving the living conditions of individuals, with a consequent reduction in social exclusion, leading to more egalitarian economic and social development.

5 THE CREDIT UNION

Credit cooperatives, by their very analogy, carry out activities that have their own characteristics and which merit a more in-depth study by those who want to know how they operate.

Therefore, in order to carry out this study, it is necessary to know, initially, some specific peculiarities of Credit Unions and the conceptual aspects of their activities.

5.1 Peculiarities

Credit unions are private sector companies, authorized to operate by the Central Bank of Brazil, created to provide financial intermediation services to their members, raising and lending funds from them, which aim not only to meet their credit needs to finance their economic activities, but also to remunerate these funds more effectively.

Although it carries out activities considered similar to those of traditional financial institutions and is, under current legislation, a financial institution, the Credit Union is not a "bank" because, unlike the latter, it has an unlimited area of operation and cannot operate with people or companies that do not belong to its membership.

Articles 9 and 10 of Chapter II of CMN Resolution 3.321/05 set out the statutory conditions for admitting members to Credit Unions:

Art. 9 Singular credit cooperatives must establish in their bylaws conditions for admitting members according to one of the following criteria: I - employees, civil servants and individuals who provide services on a non-occasional basis, of one or more legal entities, public or private, defined in the bylaws, whose activities are related, complementary or correlated, or belonging to the same economic conglomerate;

II - professionals and workers dedicated to one or more professions and activities, defined in the statute, whose objects are related, complementary or correlated;

III - people who effectively and predominantly carry out agricultural, livestock or extractive activities in the cooperative's area of operation, or are involved in catching and processing fish;

IV - small entrepreneurs, micro-entrepreneurs or micro-entrepreneurs, responsible for businesses of an industrial, commercial or service-providing nature, including activities in the rural area referred to in item III, whose annual gross revenue, at the time of the association, is equal to or less than the limit established by article 2 of Law 9.841, of October 5, 1999, and subsequent amendments;

V - entrepreneurs participating in companies linked directly to employers' unions or directly or indirectly to higher-level employers' associations, which have been in operation for at least three years when the cooperative is set up;

VI - free admission of members.

Art. 10 A single credit cooperative may provide in its bylaws for the association of:

I - its own employees and individuals who provide it with services on a non-occasional basis, who are treated as such for the corresponding legal purposes;

II - employees and individuals who provide services on a non-occasional basis to the entities associated with it and to those in whose capital it holds a direct or indirect stake;

III - retirees who, when active, met the statutory criteria for membership;

IV - parents, spouse or partner, widower, child and legal dependent and pensioner of a living or deceased member;

V - pensioners of deceased persons who met the statutory conditions for membership;

VI - legal persons, subject to the provisions of the legislation in force.

As you can see, the aforementioned Resolution lays out the conditions for membership very clearly, especially when it refers to items I and II of article 9, i.e. in other words, the Credit Union can only raise and invest funds from its members and to fulfill its related activities.

In addition, Chapter III of the same resolution establishes the special conditions relating to cooperatives with free admission of members, which will not be dealt with in this work due to the specific nature of the subject outlined.

As with other cooperative societies, Credit Unions are not-for-profit entities and, after the end of the financial year, their results/profit, if positive, are distributed to the members in proportion to their operations during the year, as determined and authorized by the general meeting.

Another special feature of credit unions is the movement of members' current sight deposit accounts, which is carried out through a banking services agreement with a particular bank in the area, chosen by the management, taking into account other services offered to meet the needs of the members and the costs charged for clearing the checks issued by them.

5.2 Specific activities

The specific activities of credit unions are nothing more than those carried out by traditional financial institutions (banks), i.e. raising and investing funds and providing services to their members, with the difference that these activities are carried out exclusively with their members and in a previously delimited area, as determined in their Articles of Association.

5.2.1 Fundraising

This is the activity through which the Credit Union raises financial resources from its members, and exclusively from them, through Demand Deposits and Term Deposits which, incorporated into the Share Capital and existing funds, aim to satisfy the needs demanded by other members, originated by loans and financing that serve to promote their activities, whether private or business.

In this respect, we must emphasize the great importance of credit cooperatives which, because of their particularity, acting regionally, are able to intermediate the resources of their members and meet their social objectives, with competitive costs well below those existing in the financial market.

This financial intermediation provides cooperative members with *comparative advantages*[3] when compared to the costs of credit operations offered by the traditional financial market and the greater ease with which they can obtain these resources, given that they are members of the institution.

In addition, these funds, earmarked for member investments, boost their activities, increasing their market share.

In this way, the members, both individuals and companies, increase their income, diluting their fixed expenses more and more and, to the extent that they make new investments with the mutual help of the cooperative, they manage to increase their *gains in scale* even more .[4]

As seen above, the Credit Union raises funds in two (2) ways:

5.2.1.1 Time Deposits

These are financial investments made by members, generally in fixed-income securities, with short or medium terms and pre or post-fixed rates, paid by the Credit Union, with a view to remunerating the funds invested.

This rate is set by the board of directors and is backed by the same type of paper and financial index in which the cooperative invests its idle funds, given that, for security reasons, it should not mismatch these rates with those it applies in the financial market. In addition, cooperative investors receive returns practically equal to those obtained by the cooperative on the financial market, when they invest their idle funds.

As a result, members feel prestigious and encouraged to invest their resources in the cooperative, since, in addition to investing in their own business (the cooperative), which promotes the growth of their social class, they also obtain higher rates of return than if they were to invest in the financial market alone, since the cooperative, by investing all of its idle resources (global value), obtains more favorable rates.

In this way, the cooperative society must constantly seek to give its members equal treatment in the best way possible. In the case of the Credit Union, it must seek, even in the long term, to remunerate the funds raised from its members in such a way as to encourage them to invest exclusively in the institution.

Furthermore, in addition to the income obtained from their financial investments, members receive another important income, based on the average balance of these investments made during the

---

3 The way in which a company obtains an advantage over another competitor in the production or marketing of products or services, due to a reduction in its operating or production costs.

4 This occurs when the company manages to increase its production and, consequently, its profitability, by reducing its costs, with the same production or operational capacity.

year/calendar year, through the distribution of the cooperative's surpluses, which are distributed by the Ordinary General Meeting, which takes place in the first three months of the following year. According to the data obtained, the cooperative surveyed has, since the second year of its activities, distributed to its members, on average, 25% to 30% more income than the normal return obtained on investments and paid by the financial market.

5.2.1.2 Sight deposits

These are the funds available in members' current accounts, which they keep in order to meet their immediate needs. In other words, it is the positive balance kept in the current account for the due provision of funds for the checks and debit orders issued by the members.

The Cash Deposits held by members in current accounts may become more or less significant over time, depending on the interest rates charged by the financial market for short-term investments. Thus, lower interest rates will make financial investments less attractive, increasing Sight Deposits and vice versa for higher interest rates.

Unlike Time Deposits, these funds are not remunerated at the time or during the investment period, i.e. they are obtained from cooperative members at zero cost.

For this reason, at first glance and as we have seen above, if part of these resources are not invested in loans and financing, they will become idle resources and, in turn, will be invested by the cooperative in the financial market and, taking into account that they have zero cost, any income obtained, whether through loans or investments, will constitute operating income, generating profit or surplus.

In order to have a better understanding of the question of "profit" or "surplus", what can be seen is that any financial investment made by the Credit Union in another member cooperative, or in its Central Office, in order to fulfill its purposes and in accordance with its social objectives, will be treated as a Cooperative Act and, therefore, its positive result should be accounted for as a surplus.

On the other hand, financial investments made in other non-associated entities will be treated as commercial activities, or middle activities, and their positive result (the difference between the income obtained minus the expenses paid to the associates for the fundraising) will have to be recorded as profit and, consequently, the taxes levied will have to be paid.

In the same way as with financial investments, members also receive a return on their sight deposits based on the average balance of their deposits for the year/calendar year, through the distribution of the cooperative's surpluses at the Annual General Meeting, which takes place in the first three months of the following year.

Also, according to data obtained by the cooperative surveyed, this yield has remained at a higher percentage than that paid by the financial market, reaching, on average, 102% to 108% of the CDI - Certificado de Depósitos Interfinanceiros (Interbank Deposit Certificate), which is credited to members' current accounts on the first working day immediately after the meeting is held.

5.2.1.3 Share Capital

In addition to Time Deposits and Demand Deposits, there are also funds from Share Capital, which in essence, in addition to having the characteristic of giving solidity to the Credit Union's business, serve as backing for the credit operations carried out to meet the needs of the members.

For a better understanding, the investments made by the members in the Share Capital will only be remunerated after the Ordinary General Meeting for the rendering of accounts for the financial year, and their remuneration is made by crediting interest to the capital, which may not exceed 12% (twelve percent) per year, as determined by § 3 of Article 24 of Law No. 5.764/71.

5.2.1.4 Funds

In addition, the cooperative also has other resources which, due to the way they are accounted for and deducted from surpluses after the annual balance sheet is closed, are recorded in Funds, as determined by Article 28, items I and II and § 1 of Law No. 5.764/71, namely:

I - A Reserve Fund intended to repair losses and meet the development of its activities, made up of at least 10% (ten percent) of the net surpluses for the financial year.

II - Technical, Educational and Social Assistance Fund, intended to provide assistance to members, their families and, when provided for in the articles of association, to the cooperative's employees, made up of at least 5% (five percent) of the net profits for the year.

§ Paragraph 1 - In addition to the funds provided for in this article, the General Meeting may create other funds, including revolving funds, with resources earmarked for specific purposes, establishing how they are to be formed, invested and liquidated.

The total of these funds, since they are not distributed to members at the time of the General Meeting for the rendering of accounts, increase the balance of the cooperative's financial investment account and, as with Share Capital and Sight Deposits, have zero cost for the cooperative, generating surpluses, which are subsequently distributed to members, as seen above.

It should also be pointed out that the resources accounted for in the Reserve Fund, FATES and other funds, should they be created, although recorded separately in the accounts, form part, together with the resources from Time Deposits and Demand Deposits, of the total resources available to the Credit Union for loans and financing to members.

5.2.2 Application of resources:

There are three (3) ways of investing the Credit Union's funds, namely

5.2.2.1 Loans

Funds invested (lent) to the Cooperative's members in order to meet their credit needs. These funds are used for Special Checks and Personal Loans.

5.2.2.1.1 Special Check

A loan intended for members via a credit limit on their individual current account, according to their needs and ability to pay.

Cooperative members are advised to use this limit on an emergency and short-term basis, i.e. if they need credit, they should go to the management office and ask for the desired amount and for the specific purpose.

This orientation is due to the fact that, precisely because it has the characteristic of emergency and short-term use, the interest on this type of credit is higher than the others practiced by the cooperative.

5.2.2.1.2 Personal loans

Loans, for which the cooperative does not require members to prove the purpose for which the funds are intended . This way, as it is a credit that has no specific purpose and has a medium and long term character, the interest rates are lower than those of the Special Cheque and slightly higher than those of other credits granted in the form of financing.

In order to release loans or financing, the cooperative must always provide the necessary guarantees to reduce the risk of possible non-payment of the commitment. These guarantees can be real (mortgage, fiduciary alienation, pledge) or by guarantee, from a member or not, but always respecting what is established in its Internal Regulations.

5.2.2.2 Financing

These are funds invested with the cooperative's members, whose characteristic, in addition to meeting specific needs (purchase of goods), is to promote the professional activity of each member, whether as a physical or legal person.

Because of their promotional nature, loans are the cooperative's most important credit instrument, since it is through them that its members are able to acquire goods on favorable terms with the financial market, which will enable them to leverage their businesses, increasing their production and, consequently, their income, as well as generating direct or indirect jobs, which will boost the economy as a whole. Loans can also be used to purchase goods for the members' personal use.

Financing can be divided into various types, such as: for the renovation, construction or acquisition of real estate; for the acquisition of vehicles, machinery and various items of equipment, consumer goods, inputs, etc., all of which are intended for the members' own use or for the development of their professional activities (individuals or companies).

The term of these loans, according to data obtained from the cooperative surveyed, can be up to 96 (ninety-six) months. In addition, depending on the type of financing taken out by the member, a grace period can be granted for the payment of the first installment, which can vary from 3 (three) to 12 (twelve) months.

According to Unicred Planalto Mèdio, the interest rates set for these types of loans only cover the cost of raising funds and administrative expenses.

In addition, members can also carry out short-term operations aimed at anticipating the inflow of funds from deals made with third parties, from whom they have obtained credit orders, such as checks, bills of exchange and promissory notes. These operations are called "discounting", and are carried out through the purchase of these assets by the cooperative, which charges the interest at the time the operation is carried out and subsequently collects it. The liquidity risk is borne by the member, who reimburses the cooperative in the event of non-payment by the third party issuing the asset.

It should be emphasized that both loans and financing are, according to the law, seen as "Cooperative Acts", since they are made to meet the credit needs of the members and, above all, for their related activities, the real reason why the Credit Cooperative was created. After all, it is through credit that the activities of the members are developed.

For simple information, when granting loans and financing to its members, the Credit Cooperative must comply with the provisions of Chapter VII "Operations and Exposure Limits per Client", Art. 28, letter "a" of Resolution No. 3. 321/05.321/05, which stipulates that a single cooperative affiliated to a central bank must be aware that no member may take out, in isolation, credit(s) that exceeds the risk exposure limit of 15% (fifteen percent) of its PR - Reference Equity. If you are not affiliated to a central bank, this limit drops to 10% of your RP.

5.2.2.3 Financial Investments

These are the cooperative's investments, made in the financial market (banks or central cooperative, member) through the purchase of short-term public securities with fixed or variable returns. Due to the nature of the activity, the cooperative's managers must ensure that these investments are as secure as possible and with the profitability necessary to cover the costs of funding.

These investments originate from idle resources, which, as mentioned above, are nothing more than the surplus of funds raised from the Credit Union's members and those belonging to the PLA -

Adjusted Net Worth (Share Capital, plus Fund(s), minus Permanent assets) and which have not been passed on to members in the form of loans or financing.

In order for the cooperative to be able to guarantee its security and solidity, without running the risk of its financial stability being affected, it must maintain a certain liquidity (idleness), in case it needs to meet requests from members to withdraw funds previously raised in Sight and Time Deposits.

The profitability of the Credit Union's financial investments follows the same criteria as those offered by the financial market to its clients. However, it should be noted that these investments come from idle resources, and that the sum of these resources, invested together and in the same financial institution, can constitute an important means of additional gain in relation to what is paid to members. This additional profit will be returned to the members at the general meeting for the rendering of accounts, when the surpluses are distributed, according to the criteria of the cooperative surveyed, as seen above, for the average balance of Demand and Term Deposits.

5.2.3 Income from services rendered

These are the revenues obtained by charging members for services rendered in the course of their activities.

The fees charged to members are intended to cover only the costs of administrative expenses incurred with: consumables, personnel, energy, security and depreciation of assets.

In addition, expenses already incurred by the Credit Union with third parties are recorded under this heading, such as: the purchase of checkbooks, which are subsequently supplied to members; the transfer of cash via credit orders (DOCs, TEDs, etc.) so that members can carry out their operations on the market.

5.3 Secondary - Auxiliary Activities:

These are the activities that the cooperative society, credit or otherwise, needs in order to carry out its core and middle businesses. This is the case, for example, with renting a property for its premises, or even, in the case of credit unions, formalizing an agreement to provide banking services, allowing members to participate in the Check and Other Paper Clearing Services (SCCOP).

In this regard, according to Becho,

> In order for the cooperative to carry out its core business and its middle business, it also needs to carry out other businesses, which are notably internal in nature, but have external effects. These are called auxiliary businesses and secondary or accessory businesses (2002, p.161).

Although this is not the main subject of this article, it is worth noting that cooperatives, especially credit cooperatives, need to carry out other activities which, under current legislation, can be considered middle or secondary activities in order to achieve their social objectives.

This is mainly the case with financial investments of its idle resources, made in other non-associated financial institutions, which, under Brazilian law, are treated as non-cooperative acts and which, if we take into account that the purpose of the operation is to preserve the value of the currency, should be treated differently, taxing only the excess gain between the income obtained from the financial investments and the expense incurred by the cooperative in raising these funds from its members.

6 UNICRED PLANALTO MÉDIO

Founded on November 5, 1993, by a group of 28 doctors, the Cooperativa de Economia e Crédito Mùtuo dos Médicos do Planalto Mèdio do Estado do Rio Grande do Sul Ltda - Unicred Planalto Médio/RS, after having its statutes approved by the Central Bank of Brazil, began its activities on June 1, 1994, with the following members in charge of its administration:

Executive Board:

- Dr. Milton Valdomiro Roos - CEO;
- Dr. Màrio Franciosi - Administrative Director;
- Dr. Adroaldo Baseggio Mallmann - Financial Director

Board of Directors:

Effective Members:

- Dr. Albino Jùlio Sciesleski
- Dr. Clebes Fagundes
- Dr. Gilberto Tubino da Silva
- Dr. Luiz Roberto Rovaris
- Dr. Mauro Frederico Sparta de Souza
- Dr. José Idilio Saggin.

Alternate Members:

- Dr. Carlos Augusto Scussel Madalosso
- Dr. Clàudio Miguel Pinto Moralles
- Dr. Roque Paulo Torres Falleiro

Supervisory Board:

Effective Members:

- Dr. Jorge Roberto de Oliveira Polita
- Dr. Luiz Carlos Trombini
- Dr. Wilmar Léo Maffezzolli

Alternate Members:

- Dr. Daniel Lara Soares

- Dr. Rubens Posser
- Dr. Antero Camisa Junior

Located at Rua Capitao Eleutério n° 665 - loja 1, provided free of charge for a period of 12 months by the company Investplan - Investimentos Imobiliârios Planalto Ltda, Unicred Planalto Médio showed early on that it would be a successful institution, as it had the massive support of its members, who already numbered 134 people, as they joined the company after it was founded, even before it began operating.

The subscribed share capital, which amounted to R$1,500.00 (one thousand five hundred reais), was paid in, as stipulated in the Articles of Association, in 60 (sixty) consecutive monthly installments of R$25.00 (twenty-five reais) each, an amount that has remained to this day. As you can see, the paid-in capital was small, but the first cooperative principle, that of **"free and voluntary membership"**, was already being felt, but enthusiastically by the doctors of the city and region, who came, if not every day, at least two or three times a week to the cooperative's headquarters, bringing their funds to be added to the demand and term deposits.

These were the first steps of an institution whose aim was much more than just to provide financial intermediation services to its members, but mainly to leverage important business and enable the medical profession to support itself with its own resources.

In the first few months, the income did not cover the expenses, but step by step, with perseverance, through weekly meetings of the Executive Board which, together with the Board of Directors, looked for new alternatives to make the institution viable, finally in September of the same year, the first positive result was achieved, in the amount of R$ 972.53 (nine hundred and seventy-two reais and fifty-three cents).

The positive results were repeated in the following months, but they were not enough to cover the deficit of the previous months, and the company ended 1994 with a negative operating result of R$819.14 (eight hundred and nineteen reais and fourteen cents), which, after using the Reserve Fund of R$759. 91 (seven hundred and fifty-nine reais and ninety-three cents), resulted in a negative final balance for the year of R$59.23 (fifty-nine reais and twenty-three cents),91 (seven hundred and fifty-nine reais and ninety-one cents), resulted in a final negative balance for the year of R$ 59.23 (fifty-nine reais and twenty-three cents), which was covered by the members after the General Meeting to render accounts held on March 14, 1995.

After this period, the following financial years were successful, with positive results that grew over time. After approval by the General Assembly, these profits were distributed to the members, always in proportion to their operations with the cooperative.

Over the years, this practice has made members feel honored and increased their relationship with the cooperative, bringing in new investments, which have given the institution enough backing to increase the volume of loans and financing, gradually reducing interest rates and, consequently, fostering, developing and making medical activity and work grow more and more.

After all, that's why a credit union is set up, to mediate the financial relations of its members, borrowing from some and lending to others, always with the aim of providing them with greater gains, or gains of scale, with even comparative advantages when compared to other financial institutions, thus fulfilling the third cooperative principle, that **of "Member economic participation"**.

One cannot fail to praise the magnificent work carried out by the management of Unicred Planalto Mèdio, who knew how to deal with the issues that arose, providing the basic conditions to reach the current stage of development and excellence of the results achieved by the cooperative.

6.1 Administration

The management of Unicred Planalto Mèdio is made up of:

- a Board of Directors, made up of 12 (twelve) members, all associates, natural persons, of whom 9 (nine) are effective and 3 (three) are substitutes, elected at a General Meeting for a term of 3 (three) years;

- an Executive Board, made up of a Chief Executive Officer, an Administrative Officer and a Chief Financial Officer, chosen by the members of the Board of Directors at the first meeting of the body following election by the General Meeting, also with a term of office of three (3) years;

- a Supervisory Board, made up of 6 (six) members, who are natural persons, 3 (three) of whom are members and 3 (three) of whom are alternates, also elected by the General Meeting, for a term of office of 1 (one) year;

- a Credit Committee, made up of three (3) associate members chosen by the Board of Directors at the first meeting of the body following election by the General Meeting, also with a mandate of three (3) years.

The Board of Directors also includes a member, whether a board member or not, chosen by the Board of Directors to represent the cooperative at the meetings of the Board of Directors of Unicred Central RS, which are held once a month.

The members of the board of directors described above are not paid any kind of remuneration for their services to the cooperative, according to the articles of association, specifically Article 63 "General and Transitional Provisions".

This is considered to be one of the main pillars of Unicred Planalto Médio's sustainability and credibility, since, in addition to substantially reducing the institution's costs, it allows members to donate their services free of charge, without any economic interest, but rather with the sole purpose of carrying forward the idea of the cooperative doctrine and spirit, it also constitutes the second cooperative principle, that **of "democratic control by the members"**.

Although, as far as anyone can tell, this is the only cooperative in the country that does not pay its directors, this is nothing new, since this practice was also part of the articles of association of the first cooperative set up by 28 selfless weavers in Rochdale, England, in 1844.

Incidentally, as described in the first paragraph of this chapter, Unicred Planalto Médio was also founded by 28 people.

Still on the subject of remuneration, according to Cattani, apud, (Potter, 1891, p.73 and 74):

> When Rochdale opened its doors in 1844, all the tasks were carried out by the managers, without being paid for it. They decided that the operation of the store should be rotated among all the members, with those who refused being fined.
>
> It was decided that no employee of the cooperative could be a member of the board of directors and no member of the board could be an employee of the cooperative. (2003, p.120)

As can be seen, this is considered to be a factor of great importance for the cooperative members; after all, development, credibility and professionalism form the main legacies built by the management of Unicred Planalto Mèdio.

6.2 Strategic actions

As described above, the management of Unicred Planalto Mèdio has managed, over time, through cohesive and participatory work, using strategically planned actions, to achieve excellent results and consolidate the cooperative's representativeness in the eyes of its members.

And it was with this spirit, and taking advantage of the credibility it had earned, that in 1997 the Board of Directors discussed and went ahead with a strategic plan that could be called daring, but with the possibility of becoming a major undertaking for the medical profession in Passo Fundo: the construction of a building that would house the city's main medical institutions in one place, in addition to Unicred's new headquarters.

After several meetings, a plot of land measuring 5,000m^2 was acquired, located on the corner of Uruguay and 10 de Abril streets.

A works committee was then chosen, made up of board members Drs. Milton Valdomiro Roos, Adroaldo Baseggio Mallmann, José Idilio Saggin, Antero Camisa Junior, Cezar Lorenzini, Clóvis Basso, Francisco Cassol de Bittencourt, Luiz Roberto Rovaris, Francisco R. Locatelli Wolff, Màrio Franciosi and Roque P. Torres Falleiro.

A new company was then set up called CONCRED - Construçoes e Incorporaçoes Ltda, with Drs. Roque Paulo Torres Falleiro, Antero Camisa Junior, Màrio Franciosi, José Idilio Saggin and Milton Valdomiro Roos as partners. The aim of the new company was to build the project that had been conceived by everyone and it was to be dissolved when the project was finished, as in fact it was.

So, step by step, under the leadership of José Idilio Saggin and Cezar Lorenzini, with the leadership of Dr. Milton Valdomiro Roos and the indispensable collaboration of all the members of the Works Committee, the Board of Directors, Directors and employees, with a lot of hard work and dedication, the work was started, completed and handed over to the members on September 22, 2000, when it was inaugurated.

The building, which has been registered under the name of Centro Comercial Unicred, has 7,025 m2 and consists of two blocks that house, in addition to the new headquarters of Unicred Planalto Médio, the following medical institutions: Unimed Planalto Médio, AMEPLAN - Associação Médica do Planalto, COOPANEST - Cooperativa dos Médicos Anestesiologistas da Regiao do Planalto Médio Ltda, COOPERTRAUMA - Cooperativa dos Médicos Ortopedistas e Traumatologistas do RGS Ltda, COOPERGISUL Cooperativa dos Médicos Ginecologistas e Obstetras do RGS Ltda, a branch of SIMERS Sindicato Médico do RGS Ltda and another 124 rooms that are used for doctors' offices, which had already been acquired by the cooperative members.

This is undoubtedly a major milestone in cooperativism, whether Unicredian or not, which, thanks to a series of consistent and innovative actions undertaken by management, which demonstrate the strength of a class, has not only won the recognition and respect of the National Unicred System and the local community, but is also the sixth and seventh cooperative principles, **"Cooperation between cooperatives"** and **"Concern for the community"**.

6.3 Education

Despite the actions undertaken, the cooperative maintains and systematically participates in an educational plan, through courses and seminars held by Unicred Central RS, aimed at training employees, managers and members.

These courses are funded by the F.A.T.E.S - Fundo de Assistência Tècnica Educacional e Social (Fund for Technical, Educational and Social Assistance) and seek to consolidate one of the most important strategic aspects of the cooperative in relation to the market, which is that managers and employees urgently need to know that they have to qualify, both in terms of knowledge and in terms of the quality of the production and services provided by the various sectors of the cooperative, because they must be prepared to face, together, the war for markets that exists in this wave of globalization, competition and concentration of wealth.

According to Schneider, "Education and training are indispensable in any institution, but in cooperatives they are a matter of survival" (2003, p.13).

Through these courses, participants have the opportunity to learn about the Unicred Cooperative System, its principles, work philosophy, forms of organization and the main branches of cooperative activity in the various regions of the country.

After all, you can't lose sight of the fact that a cooperative is different from any other society. It cultivates values that are intrinsic to human beings, such as solidarity, mutual aid, cooperation and transparency between leaders and members. This is why the issue of cooperative education must be treated with great attention, because knowledge of the doctrine will ensure the conditions for valuing the human being, specifically the cooperative member.

With this tool, Unicred Planalto Mèdio is fulfilling and will certainly have to, with concrete actions aimed at the development and training of its managers, members and employees, make this fifth cooperative principle of **"Education, training and information"** even more present.

6.4 The level of growth and development of the medical profession

This is one of the most important items in this work, because it is based on information, testimonies or numbers that we want to prove how important Credit Cooperatives are as an instrument for the growth and development of society and the classes in which they operate.

According to the information mentioned above, Unicred Planalto Mèdio has, over the years, been developing actions that allow it to get closer to its members, whether through the provision of services or its main purpose, which is financial intermediation.

The results of a questionnaire carried out among the members of Unicred Planalto Mèdio will be presented in the course of this work, in which they answered fundamental questions in order to find out about the effectiveness of the actions practiced by the cooperative with a view to the socio-economic development of the medical profession in its area of action.

However, in order to gain a broader understanding of the reasons behind the members' responses to the questions raised, it is necessary to get to know the cooperative in a broader way, by searching for data through local accounting and even through information passed on by the Unicred System, at both national and regional level, which will be demonstrated in the following items.

6.4.1 Evolution of Demand and Time Deposits

Annex A shows the evolution of Demand and Time Deposits. It shows that over the last 5 (five) years, i.e. based on the closing of the 2000 and 2005 financial years, Demand Deposits have grown by 81.26%, from 5,524 million to 10,013 million.

Demand Deposits, as we have already seen in section 5.2.1.2 of this paper, are the funds available in members' current accounts and are remunerated through the distribution of surpluses, after the General Meeting for the rendering of accounts for the year just ended, receiving important income.

One of the variables that could indicate a significant increase in this important component of the cooperative's funding is the reduction in interest rates practiced by the financial market, combined with two other factors that reduce the return on financial investments: the CPMF (0.38% on the value of the debit, if it is a financial investment) and the IRRF (15% to 22.5%, depending on how long the financial investment remains). In addition, there is another factor that is considered very important, which is participation in the cooperative's profits, based on the average balance in the current demand deposit account.

Now, if a member has funds, whether of substantial value or not, given the conditions offered by Unicred Planalto Médio, it is only interesting to make a financial investment if it is for a period of more than at least 6 (six) months. In addition, if it is an investment of less than at least 30,000 reais, since the table of investments is increasing, that is, the greater the resource, the greater the return, it is also not interesting to make the investment, because if you leave it in the current account you will be receiving a higher return than the net obtained by the financial investment. Other than that, you'll be losing income.

In terms of Time Deposits, there has also been an increase of around 393.84% in the last 5 (five) years, from 6,204 million to 30,638 million.

If we take into account that the inflation rate measured by the IPCA/IBGE for the same period was around 42.79%, we can see that there was a real growth of 38.47% in Demand Deposits and a real growth of 351.05% in Time Deposits.

Identifying this level of growth in deposits from cooperative members certainly demonstrates the level of credibility, security and satisfaction of these members, who believe in the cooperative management's ability to manage their resources.

6.4.2 Evolution of Loans/Financing

Annex B shows the figures for loans and financing from 1995 to 2005. A simple analysis of the last 5 (five) years, i.e. the period between the end of the 2000 and 2005 financial years, shows that there has been a very significant evolution in what is surely the credit cooperative's main financial intermediation factor, as it demonstrates the level of investments made by the cooperative's members. It also shows that the cooperative has certainly been achieving the social objectives for which it was created, fostering and consequently developing the medical profession in the city and region.

To be more precise, it was found that the growth rate of Loans/Financing over the last 5 years is in the order of 271.53%. In the last financial year alone, compared to the previous one (2004 to 2005), they grew by around 60.51%.

For an initial analysis of this growth in credit operations, according to data from the Central Bank of Brazil, there has been an expansion in credit over the last year, especially in the individual segment. The explanation is that, even in the face of a crisis, the country is experiencing a recovery in income and employment, which is why people feel able to make investments and, as they have no savings, seek to satisfy their needs through bank credit.

In the case of individuals, this may be a plausible explanation, since it is known that the interest rates charged by the traditional financial system are certainly more than double those charged by the cooperative credit system. According to data extracted from Anefac - the National Association of Finance, Administration and Accounting Executives, while conventional banks have an average interest rate of 5.58% per month for personal credit operations, credit cooperatives charge between 1.8 and 3.0% per month.

This is a reality that can clearly be seen in the case of individuals. Furthermore, when we analyze credit for legal entities, we see that it is very difficult to obtain funds for investments, due to the delay and bureaucracy employed by the financial system to release them, especially when it comes to investments for the acquisition of capital goods, which are necessary for generating income and employment.

It is known that the lack of access to credit is one of the obstacles to strengthening businesses, and it is in this market that Unicred Planalto Mèdio is entering and helping its members, with competitive interest rates and a lack of bureaucracy when it comes to releasing funds, because it has a unique feature of the financial system, knowledge and proximity to members, or even to the member company, which, in most cases, already has pre-approved credit lines.

There's also the fact that taking out credit from the cooperative means "paying interest" for the business itself, which will generate surpluses that will be distributed to the members, making the activity grow.

This is how Unicred Planalto Médio is growing more and more, increasing the number of members and serving all those who need it very well.

However, what can be seen is that its administrators are not concerned with the growth of the cooperative in isolation, but with strengthening the businesses of its members, who, the more investments they make, the more the cooperative will be carrying out its main activity, the promotion of credit, intensifying the activity, which will certainly grow, increasing the volume of resources that will make the reverse order, returning to the house from which it left, the Credit Cooperative.

In this respect, there are several examples of member companies making investments in order to increase their production capacity and, consequently, their economies of scale.

An example of this is the testimony of one of the state's largest medical radiology clinics, which can be found in Appendix E of this paper.

It is certainly with satisfaction that both the management of the cooperative and the member company see a business deal come to fruition. After all, this has to be the ultimate goal: to strengthen the member and the credibility of the credit institution.

6.4.3 Evolution of Gross Surpluses

The surpluses of a single credit cooperative are nothing more than the excess earnings from the management of financial intermediation, the idle resources invested in fixed-income securities at the Central and the loans and financing made to members.

The interest rates charged on credit operations by Unicred Planalto Médio, although calculated to cover the cooperative's operating costs, are also aimed at a small return, in order to cover possible operating risks caused by default and the consequent non-payment of the commitment made by a given member.

The decision taken by the management of Unicred Planalto Médio to adopt this form of action is nothing more than compliance with the fourth cooperative principle, that **of "Autonomy and Independence".**

In view of the practice determined by the calculation described above, what can be seen is that, with the substantial increase in credit, as can be seen in Annex B "Evolution of Loans/Financing", already commented on in item 6.4.2, these surpluses tend to grow. In addition, surpluses are also driven by the increase in the volume of funds raised from members, as can be seen in Annex A "Evolution of Demand and Term Deposits" and described in item 6.4.1 of this paper, and which generate surplus income.

Unicred Planalto Médio's leftovers, to outsiders who don't know the real reasons behind them, are thought to be generated by the practice of high interest rates.

In fact, the interest rates practiced, if not the lowest in the Unicred System, are among them, according to the study verified in the report "Analysis of the Unicred System's Evolution and Performance Index - April 2006", which shows the degree of risk in credit operations, the profitability of assets and operating costs.

Annex C shows Unicred Planalto Médio's "Gross Profits for the Year" for the period from 1995 to 2005. What can be seen in this report is that surpluses have grown substantially since the cooperative began operating, given that, as described above, in addition to the significant increase in the volume of funds raised and lent to members, there *has* been a low operating cost.

6.5 Regional and National Ranking

According to what has been seen so far in this paper, Unicred Planalto Mèdio has sought to develop actions aimed at serving its members since it was founded.

The way it operates, especially in terms of its target audience, is already considered distinctive, given that, in regional terms, it is still the only Unicred Credit Cooperative that has not opened up its membership to other categories of health professionals.

According to statements made by its management, this is an option that continues to be defended by its membership, of being a cooperative focused solely on serving the medical profession in the city and region.

Although this decision continues to be defended, the cooperative, according to the statements made in section 6.4 and the figures presented in Annexes A, B and C of this work, continues to grow constantly, with a greater emphasis on the last few years, which has been significant.

This information is confirmed when we analyze the latest consolidated report of the Unicred System, with base date April 2006, which presents all the accounting information of Brazil's Unicred Credit Cooperatives, which shows that Unicred Planalto Médio, among the 132 Unicred cooperatives, occupies the following positions in the Ranking:

- Demand Deposits: 9ª place, with 10,483 million;
- Time Deposits: 10th place, with 36,483 million;
- Net Worth: 30th place, with 5.955 million;
- Total Loans: 15th place, with 22,107 million;

In the General Classification, by total resources, based on the numbers presented above, it is 15th in the country.

On the other hand, not in order to make comparisons, but simply to place the Unicred surveyed in the context of the Unicred System in Brazil, it is important to present some data, which will be seen below:

Unicred Planalto Mèdio is the only cooperative among those ranked up to 19th place to have less than 1000 members. More precisely, it has 617 members. This is a relevant fact if we take into account that its target audience is infinitely smaller than the cooperative ranked 1st, which has 4,774 members, or even when we look at the one ranked 14th, with 3,018 members.

What's even more relevant and striking is the volume of resources per member, because although it came 15th in the General Classification, it has the highest value in this indicator, R$85,770.00 per member. To give an example, the cooperative in 1st place has R$37,260.00 per member, which is less than half.

If we look at the distribution of surpluses, while Unicred Planalto Médio would distribute, in a simple division, R$1,993.00 (one thousand, nine hundred and ninety-three reais) to each member, the cooperative in 1st place would distribute only R$918.00 (nine hundred and eighteen reais), in other words, less than half.

Furthermore, if we look at the level of development of loans/financing, in the period analyzed between 31/12/2005 and 30/04/2006, the base date for the report, while Unicred Planalto Médio grew by 15.87%, the cooperative ranked 1st grew by only 4.91%, or less than 1/3.

In terms of efficiency, Unicred Planalto Médio is, along with other cooperatives in the system, ranked 1st in the state and in the country, as can be seen in Appendix D of this paper. This item takes into account general evolutionary aspects, which are given a score.

As can be seen, this is a collection of positive information that makes the cooperative in question stand out in the Unicred System, as well as increasing its credibility with its members.

However, comparisons aside, what remains is that both the Unicred surveyed and the other Unicred's in the system have been showing their strength, given the volume of their operations, making the entire medical profession in the country, when using their services, have the cooperative as their business partner, so that they can increase their earnings.

7 ANALYSIS OF THE RESULTS OF THE SURVEY OF UNICRED PLANALTO MÉDIO MEMBERS

The aim of this chapter is to find out how Unicred Planalto Médio has been operating, as well as the participation and satisfaction levels of its members in relation to the services it provides.

It also aims to answer some of the questions raised in this paper, more precisely in Chapter 1 - "Identifying the Problem and its Justification", by analyzing the results of the survey. The survey of members can be found in Appendix A of this paper.

Obviously, over the years, from time to time, all the work carried out must undergo a diagnosis. For this reason, consulting the clients directly involved with the company is an essential task in order to show, if necessary, new paths to be taken by management.

It is extremely important to know what customers think about the company's performance, so that its managers can reflect on the direction it is taking and, most likely, by knowing this diagnosis, they can introduce some changes to that direction, with a view to improving the services offered, which could consequently lead to better results.

To carry out the survey, 103 questionnaires were printed and answered between May 22 and June 9, 2006, and distributed to members as follows:

- 70 questionnaires were handed out at random to cooperative members who came to the cooperative to carry out transactions;

- 30 questionnaires were delivered to buildings where members have doctors' surgeries. These questionnaires were handed out at the entrance to the buildings so that the advisors could randomly ask for answers.

- 3 questionnaires were given to the company directors to answer.

Of the total number of questionnaires handed out, 88 responses were obtained, which is why only 15 of those handed out at doctors' surgeries came back with a response.

The tables below show the tabulation of the data obtained from the answers to questions 1 to 5 on the satisfaction of cooperative members, which we will now analyze:

Table - 1

Questions	No answer	% of Responses									
		1	2	3	4	5	6	7	8	9	10
1							2,27	5,68	19,32	25,00	47,73

2	1,13					1,14	2,27	6,82	12,50	21,59	54,55
3	1,13			2,27		2,27	1,14	10,23	10,23	25,00	47,73
4	1,13					3,41	1,14	3,41	25,00	27,27	38,64
5								5,68	21,59	26,14	46,59

Source: Questionnaires, June 2006 - Unicred Planalto Médio RS

Table - 2

Questions	**Levels**				
	7	**8**	**9**	**10**	**Total %**
1	5,68	19,32	25,00	47,73	**97,73**
2	6,82	12,50	21,59	54,55	**95,46**
3	10,23	10,23	25,00	47,73	**93,19**
4	3,41	25,00	27,27	38,64	**94,32**
5	5,68	21,59	26,14	46,59	**100,00**
Average	**31,82**	**88,64**	**25,00**	**47,05**	**96,14**

Source: Questionnaires, June 2006 - Unicred Planalto Médio RS

7.1 Results and analysis of the satisfaction survey - Tables 1 and 2

In accordance with the methodology applied in the survey and given that the answers from levels 1 to 6 reached a maximum of 6.81% (question 3) as can be seen in Table 1, only the answers from levels 7 to 10 will be analyzed, according to the data extracted from Table 2, where it can be seen that:

a-) according to the sum of the percentages described in question 1, 97.73% of members believe that the cooperative has been achieving the objectives for which it was created;

b-) when analyzing the percentages described in question no. 2, 95.46% of the members say that the cooperative is competitive in terms of interest rates, both in attracting and granting credit;

c-) Regarding credit promotion, question 3, 93.19% of members believe that the cooperative is able to leverage and develop medical activities;

d) In the sum of the percentages answering question 4, 94.32% of the members were satisfied with the way in which the services provided by the cooperative in financial intermediation are being carried out;

e) According to question 5, which referred to the activities carried out by the cooperative as a whole, 100% of the members were satisfied;

f-) When all the percentages are added together, 96.14% of the answers are between levels 7 and 10, which indicates a high level of satisfaction with the cooperative's activities;

7.2 Results and analysis of the participation survey

With regard to question 6, 38.64% of the members who answered the questionnaire were interested in participating in the management of the cooperative at some point, demonstrating a good level of interest on the part of the members.

In question 7, 42.05% of the members reported that they exclusively invest their funds in the cooperative.

Still on the subject of question 7, 57.95% of the members reported that they do not invest their funds exclusively in the cooperative.

Of these, although they believe that the cooperative has been achieving the objectives for which it was created and show a high degree of satisfaction, on average they invest only 59.82% of their funds in the cooperative, i.e. 40.18% of these members' funds are in other financial institutions.

a-) a member says that he invests 100% of his funds in the Ibovespa.

In question 8, 100% of the members said that they believe in the management capacity of the current directors and staff.

In analyzing the responses, the diagnosis is that Unicred Planalto Médio has been achieving its objectives, and the level of responses demonstrates the high degree of credibility and reliability in the management of resources.

However, administrators need to think again, especially when it comes to the financial transactions of cooperative members, since only 57.95% of those who answered the questionnaire reported that only 59.82% of their funds are transferred to the cooperative. This information shows that there is a need for more intensive work, especially in terms of providing guidance and education to cooperative members, showing them the advantages that the cooperative offers.

In addition, it is important to inform members that the resources invested in the cooperative provide greater business leverage, which will consequently result in better returns for investors. With more resources, the cooperative will have greater and better conditions to promote credit, favoring the growth of the class.

The most important diagnosis to be made from the questionnaire is that, despite all the advantages offered by the cooperative and the actions it has been taking with a view to the socio-economic development of the medical profession in the city and region, there is still a market to be worked on, especially with regard to finding those members who do not work exclusively with the cooperative.

CONCLUSION

After all the considerations and information provided about the Unicred Planalto Médio Credit Cooperative, it is worth highlighting what the work has shown: that the financial support given to members has been a preponderant factor, constituting an important development tool for the medical profession, especially in terms of increasing its business.

In addition, the conclusion of this work shows that Credit Cooperatives, in addition to being a reaction to the threats and challenges of the globalized world, are a concrete alternative for those who unite with the aim of reducing financial costs, boosting their business, increasing gains in scale, productivity indices, quality, etc?

The future offers no prospects for companies and sectors of the economy that are vulnerable. Therefore, it is more than necessary to know that Credit Cooperatives are capable of overcoming the inertia of the market, through solidarity and awareness, above collective interests.

This work has fulfilled its objective, because by presenting issues relating to Credit Cooperatives and showing how they operate, it has shown that this market segment is very important and will certainly be able to occupy an even greater place in the Brazilian economic scene, along with the other business segments, and make a real contribution to the social and economic development of all social classes.

For this reason, it is essential to get people to incorporate a culture of cooperation into their lives, working together and focusing on results, because only in this way will they be able to overcome the challenges imposed by the market.

One thing is certain: everyone agrees that our country's main problem is its ability to generate jobs and income. This work has certainly provided the solution. Credit Cooperatives are a concrete alternative for improving life and the country's economy, as they are able to provide investments at much lower interest rates than those practiced by the financial market.

In addition, Credit Unions in Brazil have what can be called an extra ingredient. They go beyond the financial issue to become, as presented in the paper, an instrument of economic and social development.

The current Brazilian government has woken up to this potential and has paid special attention to the sector, encouraging growth and the expansion of new units.

To better exemplify this, we can observe the advances in legislation that came about with the publication of Resolutions 3.058/02 and 3.106/03, the latter revoked by Resolution 3.321/05, which allowed the constitution and transformation of Credit Cooperatives of a certain social class into free admission ones.

Finally, what remains to be seen is that credit unions today occupy a space not served by traditional financial institutions. Certainly, because of the way they operate and the market they are conquering, they are forcing greater competition with banks, especially when they lend money at lower interest rates to their members.

BIBLIOGRAPHICAL REFERENCES

BRUM, Argemiro. **Brazilian economic development**. Petrópolis: Vozes, 2000.

CATTANI, Antonio David. **Work and technique: a** critical dictionary. Petrópolis/Porto Alegre: Vozes. University Press, 1997.

. **The other economy**. Porto alegre. Veraz. 2003

CARRION, Raul; VIZENTINI, Paulo. **Globalization, neoliberalism, privatization:** who decides this game. Porto Alegre, Editora da Universidade, 1997.

LESBAUPIN, Ivo. **The dismantling of the nation**. Petrópolis, Vozes, 1999.

COSTA, Achyles Barcelos da. Economic development in Joseph Schumpeter's vision. In: **Cadernos IHU Idéias**, Sao Leopoldo, Unisinos, year 4, n° 47, 2006.

BECHO, Renato Lopes. Elements of Positive Law. 1. ed. Sao Paulo: Dialética, 2002.

BECHO, Renato Lopes. Taxation of Cooperatives. 2. ed. Sao Paulo: Dialética, 1999.

NAMORADO, Rui. The Cooperative Principles. 1. ed. Fora do Texto: Coimbra, 1995.

PERIUS, Vergilio Frederico. Cooperativism and the Law. 1. ed. Unisinos: Sao Leopoldo, 2001.

SCHNEIDER, José Odelso. Democracia, Participaçao e Autonomia Cooperativa. 2. ed. Unisinos: Sao Leopoldo, 2003.

APPENDIX A

Dear Member!

With a view to the final development of the Monograph Work, in the Post-Graduate course in Cooperative Management, taught by UNISINOS, which I am preparing, I ask the special favor of answering the questionnaire below, returning it to Unicred's headquarters by 10/06/2006.

Questionnaire:

For questions 1 to 5, an evaluation score should be given, ranging from 1 to 10, by marking "X" in the corresponding field.

1) Do you believe that the cooperative has achieved the objectives for which it was created?

1	2	3	4	5	6	7	8	9	10

2) In relation to the local financial system (banks), is Unicred Planalto Médio competitive in terms of interest rates, both in terms of funding (financial investments) and in terms of granting credit (loans and financing)?

1	2	3	4	5	6	7	8	9	10

3) And in relation to credit promotion, what rating do you give the cooperative as an entity capable of leveraging and developing medical activities, both for individuals and legal entities?

1	2	3	4	5	6	7	8	9	10

4) How satisfied are you with the way the financial intermediation services provided by the cooperative are being carried out?

1	2	3	4	5	6	7	8	9	10

5) Overall, in relation to the activities carried out by the cooperative, what are your

level of satisfaction with it?

1	2	3	4	5	6	7	8	9	10

For questions 6 to 8, answer Yes or No by marking "X" in the corresponding box.

6) Are you interested in taking part in the management of the cooperative at some point?

Yes No

7) Do you invest your funds exclusively in the cooperative?

Yes No

If you don't apply exclusively, enter the approximate percentage of the total in the field below

its resources, which it invests in Unicred. _____ %

8) Do you believe in the management capacity of the cooperative on the part of the current directors and employees?

Yes No

Thank you for your attention.

Avelino Marcos Guarienti - Manager Unicred Planalto Médio RS

ANNEX

ANNEX A

EVOLUTION OF DEMAND AND TERM DEPOSITS

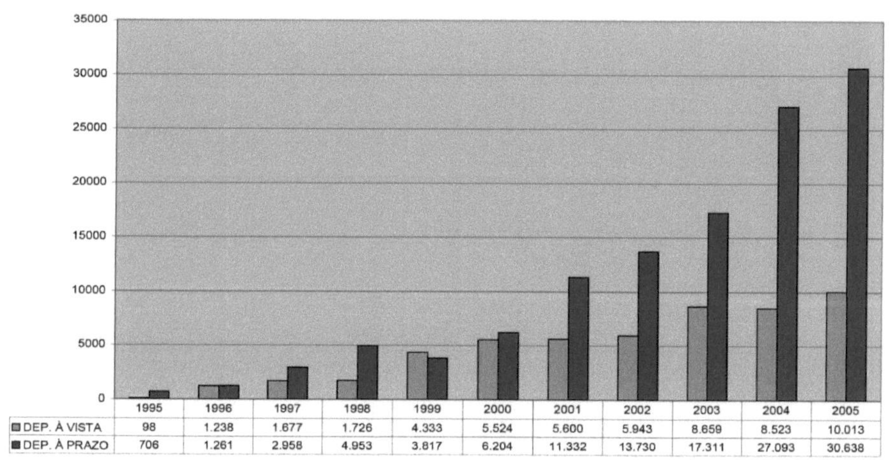

	1995	1996	1997	1998	1999	2000	2001	2002	2003	2004	2005
DEP. À VISTA	98	1.238	1.677	1.726	4.333	5.524	5.600	5.943	8.659	8.523	10.013
DEP. À PRAZO	706	1.261	2.958	4.953	3.817	6.204	11.332	13.730	17.311	27.093	30.638

ANNEX B

DEVELOPMENT OF LOANS - FINANCIAL YEARS (IN THOUSAND R$)

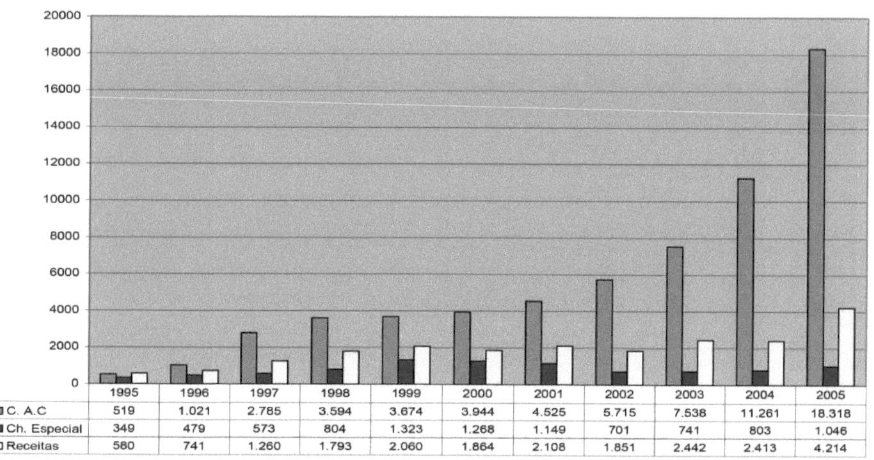

	1995	1996	1997	1998	1999	2000	2001	2002	2003	2004	2005
C. A.C	519	1.021	2.785	3.594	3.674	3.944	4.525	5.715	7.538	11.261	18.318
Ch. Especial	349	479	573	804	1.323	1.268	1.149	701	741	803	1.046
Receitas	580	741	1.260	1.793	2.060	1.864	2.108	1.851	2.442	2.413	4.214

ANNEX C

CHANGES IN GROSS SURPLUS FOR THE YEAR

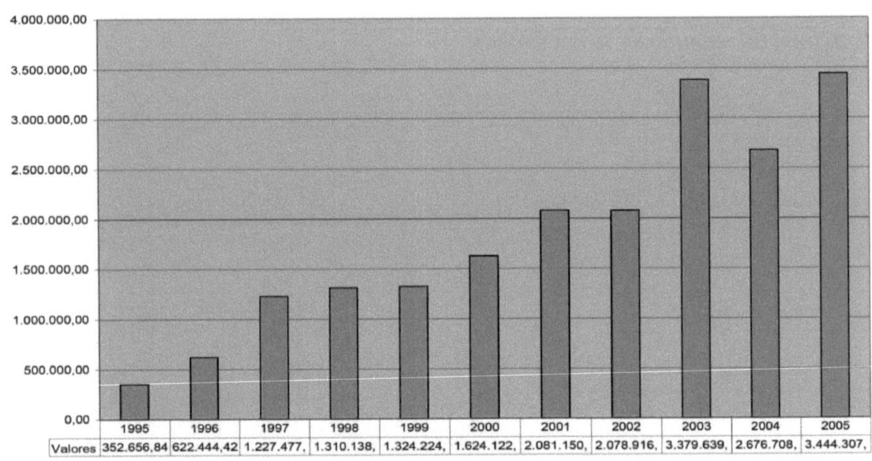

ANNEX D - Ranking of Unicreds in Rio Grande do Sul

		TAMANHO							EFICIÊNCIA										EVOLUÇÃO							Rating		GERAL		
	UNICRED'S	1	2	3	4	SOMA	C.R	C.G.	5	6	7	8	9	10	11	SOMA	C.R	C.G	12	13	14	15	SOMA	C.R	C.G	16	T.P	C.R	C.G	C.G.*
	CRUZ ALTA	92	41	40	65	238	11	73	16	40	29	5	25	25	45	185	17	103	25	4	0	10	39	18	115	25	487	15	93	89
	NORDESTE -CX SUL	113	120	113	112	458	3	17	31	35	45	25	25	45	36	242	12	55	6	21	3	7	37	20	119	45	782	3	22	19
	PORTO ALEGRE	123	130	123	129	505	1	5	45	35	45	15	35	35	45	255	10	40	17	18	6	22	63	6	78	45	868	2	12	11
R	MISSÕES/SANGELO	99	104	92	89	384	5	31	16	35	45	45	35	45	16	237	13	57	25	16	0	7	48	15	106	35	704	7	38	39
I	PLANALTO MÉD -P.FUNDO	124		103	118	468	2	15	45	35	45	45	45	45	45	305	1	1	9	25	3	25	62	8	84	45	880	1	10	9
O	VALE DAS ANTAS -CASCA	115	12	63	52	242	10	72	45	35	45	45	45	45	36	296	4	9	25	7	3	25	60	10	89	35	633	9	62	49
	VALE DO CAÍ	23	47	22	43	135	19	103	23	35	5	0	45	25	45	178	18	105	25	18	15	4	62	8	84	10	385	19	112	119
G	REGIÃO DA PRODUÇÃO	112	1	43	55	211	12	81	45	35	45	45	35	35	45	285	6	16	17	0	3	19	39	18	115	45	580	12	74	58
R	ERECHIM	109	55	44	73	281	9	60	45	35	37	45	45	45	16	268	8	34	0	25	0	25	50	13	101	25	624	10	64	60
A	IJUI	100	83	88	88	359	7	37	45	35	37	45	45	45	45	297	3	8	25	25	12	13	75	3	53	45	776	5	24	22
N	REGIÃO DA FRONTEIRA-LIV	25	40	45	68	178	15	93	31	37	5	15	25	15	36	164	20	117	14	4	9	16	43	17	111	15	400	18	106	101
D	V. TAQUARI E R. PARDO	89	97	114	105	405	4	24	8	35	29	45	45	45	16	223	14	74	11	25	0	10	46	16	108	45	719	6	33	30
E	PELOTAS	127	63	89	98	377	6	32	45	35	45	45	35	45	45	295	5	12	25	25	9	4	63	6	78	45	780	4	23	23
	SANTA ROSA	29	62	36	16	143	18	101	16	35	37	5	15	45	36	189	15	100	0	0	0	25	25	21	124	25	382	20	113	109
D	LITORAL SUL-RIO GRANDE	42	51	33	42	168	16	95	0	35	37	0	45	25	45	187	16	102	0	25	0	0	25	21	124	35	415	17	102	102
O	VALE D. SINOS - NH	117	76	83	82	358	8	40	45	35	45	15	35	35	36	246	11	51	25	0	15	10	50	13	101	25	679	8	47	44
	VALE DO JACUI	10	9	2	2	23	22	131	0	24	29	0	0	0	36	89	23	132	25	7	22	13	67	4	67	10	189	23	132	132
S	CENTRO JACUÍ	37	39	20	32	128	20	106	45	35	37	15	45	35	45	257	9	39	25	18	25	25	93	2	21	45	523	14	88	95
U	BAGE	93	14	26	15	148	17	100	45	35	45	35	45	35	45	285	6	16	25	0	9	25	59	11	90	45	537	13	81	83
L	SANTA MARIA	45	60	31	62	198	13	85	16	35	5	15	45	25	36	177	19	106	0	0	0	25	25	21	124	35	435	16	99	84
	FRONTEIRA OESTE	108	15	32	35	190	14	87	45	35	45	45	45	45	45	305	1	1	25	0	25	16	66	5	68	45	606	11	68	69
	SIVEICRED-RS	8	8	13	13	42	21	128	23	37	5	5	35	0	36	141	21	125	9	13	22	13	57	12	95	10	250	21	130	130
	COOPNORE	3	5	1	1	10	23	132	0	45	5	0	0	0	45	95	22	131	25	25	25	25	100	1	1	5	210	22	131	131

ANNEX E

History of Clinica Kozma and its relationship with Unicred Planalto Mèdio

Medicine has undergone transformations over the years and, depending on the medical specialty, the advances have been greater or lesser. For those who follow the development of medical science, either by virtue of their profession or by mere scientific curiosity, there is no doubt that radiology is one of the branches that has progressed the most, especially since the 70s.

The speed and volume of these changes have led to a significant shift in the role of this medical specialty, not only in the qualification of its professionals, but also of these with professionals from other fields, whether medical or not.

Today, radiology costs represent between 6 and 10% of all healthcare costs and its use is set to grow, due to the spectacular results it has already produced and those it will produce with the incorporation of new methods and technologies, the prestige it has acquired in the eyes of doctors and patients and due to the relative comfort of carrying out examinations when compared to other types of complementary tests.

In line with these concepts, Clinica Kozma was founded and opened on January 2, 1977. Its name is a tribute to the illustrious radiologist Dr. Miguel Kozma, one of the pioneers of the specialty in the highlands and middle plateau of the state.

For sixteen years, Clinica Kozma was located at 480 Avenida Brasil, in the Edificio Kozma, the original office of the professional who lent it its name. In 1993, Clinica Kozma moved to the medical heart of Passo Fundo, at 793 Rua Teixeira Soares.

In this new phase, Clinica Kozma has incorporated imaging methods that broadened the horizons of medical diagnosis in the 1980s and 1990s, such as ultrasound, high-resolution mammography and computed tomography. Its pioneering automatic processing and total computerization of the service is the result of a vision that there is a need to adapt medical care to the needs of patients who, in addition to the quality of the services, seek agility in care and speed in obtaining results.

More recently, the clinic has had its physical area extended by 800 square meters, where helical computed tomography, nuclear magnetic resonance, nuclear medicine service, specialized dental radiology service and a large auditorium for medical-scientific meetings have been installed.

Clinica Kozma is currently established in 2200 square meters of built area and has around

100 employees including technicians, attendants, secretaries and auxiliary staff, currently with a total of eleven professionals and their team of medical and dental radiologists, providing services to doctors and patients from more than 143 municipalities in the north of Rio Grande do Sul and west of Santa Catarina, also counting on extensions in the form of partnerships with the Hospital da Cidade de Passo Fundo and the Hospital de Caridade de Erechim.

At the end of 2002 until March 2003, the company experienced serious financial difficulties and had to obtain funds from the financial market, more precisely from Unicred Planalto Mèdio, in order to resolve its financial situation. After tireless negotiations with other financial institutions, it was from Unicred Planalto Mèdio that we obtained the necessary resources and the viability to resume the organization's sustainable growth.

After this injection of funds, the company was able to restructure itself and continue its activities.

In 2005 and 2006, Unicred Planalto Médio was once again instrumental in the company's growth. With the availability of resources, the company was able to acquire a new 4,000m2 plot of land, where the new facilities are planned, as well as renewing its equipment structure, having acquired new state-of-the-art magnetic resonance equipment, a digital mammography machine, found only in large, modern reference centers in the field of imaging diagnostics, as well as expanding our physical structure by another 700m2.

With the partnership found at Unicred Planalto Mèdio, the data is extremely favorable, as in 3 years the company has doubled its turnover, tripled the number of employees and is expanding its operations to the city of Erechim/RS and Pato Branco/PR.

With the investments, the company plans to increase its net operating revenue by approximately 40%, and overall growth in the order of 50% of its current figures.

In view of the above, we can say that Unicred Planalto Mèdio, over the last three years, is an example of a financial institution that clearly achieves its objectives, promoting medical activity and facilitating the day-to-day life of its member companies.

The ease of access to resources and the convenience of the structure as a whole means that we have the confidence and credibility to rely on Unicred at all times, good or bad. Furthermore, even with the continuity of the current policy, we are sure that we will always be a partner in the development and growth of our region, offering our clients the best services in the health area.

Sincerely,

Anderson Luis Sudrè
Administrative Manager

The Board

Printed by Books on Demand GmbH, Norderstedt / Germany